THE
JESUS STORY

GOD'S PROMISE

CLEAR & SIMPLE MEDIA

A Simple Word

If you would like to know more about who we are and what we do, visit our website at www.asimpleword.org

The people who wrote this book are all people who follow Jesus. We wrote it so that you can hear his story. And we hope, that after you read it, you will want to follow him too.

CHAPTER ONE

Who is Jesus?

If you have heard anything about Jesus, you probably have thought about that question. But not everyone answers that question in the same way.

For example, many people say that Jesus spoke for God. They say that Jesus was a prophet. We believe that too, but we believe that Jesus was much more than a prophet.

Other people say that Jesus was a wise man, a teacher. During his life, Jesus taught many helpful things. We believe that as well, but we also believe that Jesus was much more than a wise teacher.

Some people say that Jesus was a good example to follow. He lived the type of life that all people should try to live. We believe that too. If we all lived as Jesus did, we would be better people. The world would be a better place. But we believe that Jesus was much more than a good example.

We believe that Jesus was more than a prophet, a wise man, and a good example. We believe that Jesus is the Son of God. We believe that, when Jesus was born, God became a man. And we believe that, because he loved us, he came to rescue us from our biggest problem.

One of the men who wrote about Jesus said it this way:

> *God loved the world so much that he gave his only Son, Jesus. God did this so that whoever puts his trust in Jesus will not perish but will have a life that lasts forever.*

CHAPTER TWO

So, what do you believe about Jesus?

You may have some questions if you have never heard anyone speak about Jesus in this way.

"Why do I need to be rescued?"

"What did Jesus come to rescue the world from?"

We find the answer to these questions in the Bible. The story starts in the first book of the Bible called Genesis. And, as you will see, it continues through the Bible to the last chapter.

CHAPTER THREE

Adam to Abraham

The Bible begins with God. And God made everything. He made the heavens. He made the earth. And he filled the heavens and the earth with good things. Then, God made a man named Adam. And he made a woman named Eve. He put them in a beautiful garden. They could eat the fruit of every tree in the garden. They had everything that they needed. And everything that they had was a good gift from God.

But God told them that there was one thing that they could not do. They could not eat from one of the trees in the middle of the garden. If they ate from that tree, they would die. Adam and Eve trusted that God was wise and good. So they did not eat from that tree.

Until one day, a serpent came to the garden. Satan, the Evil One, used the serpent to tell Eve a lie. He told her to eat the fruit that God told them not to eat. He told her that nothing bad would happen to them. If they ate from the tree, they would be wise and learn things that only God knows.

And Adam and Eve chose to believe that lie.

They chose not to obey God. They ate the fruit. When they did, they turned away from the God who made them. And they soon found out that what the serpent told them was a lie. Instead of becoming wise, they felt guilty, afraid, and ashamed.

> He made them clothes to cover them. And God made them a **promise**.

But God loved the man and woman that he made. And he did not leave them. He returned to the garden. He spoke to them. He made them clothes to cover them. And God made them a **promise**.

God said that they would have a son. He said that one day, the serpent would bruise the heel of the son. But that son would crush the head of the serpent, the Evil One.

But, because they had sinned, they could not live with God in the place he made for them. So God sent them away from the garden. And they could never go back there again.

After Adam and Eve left the garden, many things happened. They had children. But, like Adam and Eve, their children did not honor God. They sinned. One of their sons even killed his brother. Soon their children had children, and their children's children had children. And the number of people on the earth grew and grew. But as more people began to live on the earth, they became more and more evil.

CHAPTER FOUR

Abraham to Moses

Many years went by. But God did not stop caring about the people that he had made. He had a plan to rescue them. God chose a man named Abram and made him a **promise**. He told Abram that he would make him great. God would give him a land of his own. God would give him a son. And all the nations on the earth would be blessed because of Abram. Then God changed Abram's name to Abraham.

Later, Abraham did have a son. His name was Isaac. Isaac became a man and had a son named Jacob. Jacob grew to be a man and had 12 sons. God changed Jacob's name and called him Israel. And the sons of Jacob became known as the children of Israel.

After many years, there was a time when there was no food in Abraham's land. So Jacob and his family, the children of Israel, moved to Egypt. Things went well for them there. But after many years, a new king ruled Egypt who did not like Jacob's family. He made them slaves. The children of Israel lived in Egypt for 400 years. But God did not forget the **promises** he had made to Abraham.

CHAPTER FIVE

Moses to David

One day, God came to speak to a man named Moses. God told Moses that he was to lead the children of Israel back to the land that he gave Abraham. The king of Egypt did not want that to happen. This was not going to be an easy task. But God **promised** to help Moses. And because God did many amazing things through Moses, the king of Egypt let them go. After the children of Israel left Egypt, God **promised** he would be their God and they would be his people. He would bless them and give them the land that he had given to Abraham. They would become a great nation, just as he had **promised**.

While Moses was their leader, God made new **promises** to the children of Israel. He also gave Israel laws to help them live in ways that pleased God. When they followed God's laws, he would bless them. If they did not follow them, God would not bless them. But sometimes the people did not obey God. So, God made a way that, when they had done wrong, they could be forgiven. He made a way that they could be right with him again.

When someone did wrong, they were not to hide what they had done. They were to confess that wrong before God. Then they were to bring an animal to the priest as a sacrifice. Because of the sacrifice, God would forgive them for what they had done. The animal died so that the one who sinned could live.

Moses led the people for many years through many troubles. And the people did get back to the land God gave them. They lived there for a long time. God was with them. He sent men and women called judges to lead them. But the people did not always follow the leaders that God sent. They did not always follow the laws God gave them through Moses. They did many things that did not please God in those days. And one day they decided that they did not want to follow the judges any more. They wanted a king instead.

> God was with them.

CHAPTER SIX

David to Exile

So God gave them what they wanted, a king. But the first king did not follow God. So God gave them a second king. His name was David. God made a special **promise** to David just as he had with Abraham and Moses. God **promised** that he would make David's name great. He **promised** that one of David's sons would be the king of Israel. And this son would also become the king of all the nations of the world. This son's kingdom would continue forever.

While David was king, God blessed Israel. The kingdom was strong. The nation was safe.

David had a son named Solomon. Just before David died, Solomon became king. God made him great like his father. Solomon built a special house for God called the temple. The temple was a place where the people could come to worship God. But Solomon did not love God as his father David did. He did many things that did not please God. He even allowed the people in his kingdom to follow other gods. So when Solomon died, there was trouble in the land of Israel. The kingdom broke apart. The nation was divided. Did God forget his **promise**?

> God would not forget the **promises** he had made.

In those days, God used special men and women called prophets to speak to his people. God sent them to tell the people to stop following other gods. The prophets said that if they did not return to God, God would punish them. God would let their enemies overcome them and take away their land. The people would be made to live in places that were far away from home.

For many years, the prophets warned the people. But they did not listen. So God sent armies to fight against Israel. Those armies were stronger than Israel. And, just as the prophets had said, they took the people away from the land.

It was a very sad time. But God did not forget his people. He sent prophets to comfort them. The prophets said that God would not forget the **promises** he had made. They would return to the land that he had **promised** Abraham.

CHAPTER SEVEN

Exile to Return

For many years, the people of God lived in exile. But, one day, just as the prophets had said, God did bring the people back to their land. When they arrived, war had broken many things. But the people were happy to come home. So they began to build again. They built homes to live in. They worked to repair the temple. They rebuilt the walls of the city. Leaders taught them God's laws again. And the people worshiped God.

But life was not easy for those who returned. They were not a great nation any longer. They had no army. They had no king. But God sent prophets to give them hope. The prophets told them that God had not forgotten the **promises** that he had made to Abraham, Moses, and David. God would send someone to rescue them. The people began to call this **promised** one, the Messiah. And God always keeps his **promises.**

CHAPTER EIGHT

Return to Jesus

So the people waited. For almost 400 years, there was no new word from God. No new prophets spoke. No kings from David's family came to rule.

Until one day, a most surprising thing happened. An angel appeared to a young virgin named Mary. The angel told her that God was about to do a miracle. Mary would have a son. This son would have no man as his father. He would be called the Son of God. He was to be given the name Jesus. Her son would sit on the throne of David. He would be the one whom God had **promised** - the Messiah. He would be king over his people forever.

Soon, Mary gave birth to a son. God had kept his **promise**. And the boy grew taller and wiser each year. And when he was about 30 years old, he began to travel from place to place talking about the kingdom of God. He chose some men to be his followers. They went with him wherever he went. They heard him say and do many wonderful things. He made blind people see again. He made sick people well again. He even touched people who had died and made them live again. The men who followed him watched all of this. And they saw that in everything he did, he did nothing evil. He did not sin.

Many people were happy to see what Jesus did. They loved to listen to him teach and hear his stories. But some people did not like Jesus. Many of the leaders became angry with him. They began to hate him.

They said that the things that Jesus was doing did not come from God. They said that Jesus claimed to do what only God could do. He even said he could forgive sins. Jesus said things that made people think that he was God. The leaders became so angry with Jesus that they decided to kill him.

Jesus knew what the leaders were planning. So he called his followers together. He wanted to have a special meal with them. While they were eating together, he told them what would happen. Angry men would take hold of Jesus. They would hand him over to soldiers. The soldiers would kill him. They would nail Jesus to a cross, and there, Jesus would die. But he told his followers that they should not be afraid. God would bring Jesus back to life again. And that is what happened.

> On the cross, God showed his love for the world.

But Jesus did not die only because men were angry with him. Jesus died to do something much more important. On the cross, God showed his love for the world. Soldiers did not take Jesus' life from him. Jesus gave his life as a sacrifice so that we could be right with God. Jesus, himself, took the punishment that a world of sinful people deserved.

The one who never sinned died to make a way for sinners to be forgiven. And just as Jesus had said he would, on the morning of the third day after his death, he came out of the place where he had been buried - alive. Jesus had defeated death. God brought him back to life to show that Jesus was who he claimed to be. He is the only one who can give us life. He had done what he **promised** to do.

After Jesus came back to life, he spent some time teaching the men and women who believed in him. He told them that he would go to be with God soon. But one day, he would return. And when he returns, he will right every wrong. He will fix everything that is broken. And his kingdom will never end. But until then, they must not be afraid, because he would not leave them alone. He would send the Holy Spirit to be with them and to help them. After the Spirit came, they were to go everywhere and tell everyone the good news.

And what is that good news? All people have sinned, and their sins have separated them from God. But Jesus, the Son of God has come. He lived a perfect life. He died and is alive again. On the cross he took the place of sinners. He took the curse that their sin deserves upon himself. When sinners put their trust in who Jesus is and what he has done, God forgives them. God welcomes them into his family as one of his own. They will begin a new life that lasts forever.

After Jesus finished saying these things, God took him up to heaven through the clouds. Then, the followers did what Jesus told them to do. They went everywhere they could go and told everyone they met about Jesus.

> When sinners put their trust in who Jesus is and what he has done, God forgives them. God welcomes them into his family as one of his own.

CHAPTER NINE

Jesus to Now

Many years later, God came to one of the first men to follow Jesus. His name was John. God gave him a dream about the future. He showed him that life would be hard for those who follow Jesus. God told him that, in the days to come, Satan will fight against God. Satan will lie to many people. But John was not to be afraid. For Jesus will return to earth. He will judge the world and punish Satan and the people who followed Satan. Then God will gather his people. And they will be with him forever. God will make a new heaven and a new earth. He will rule the nations. His glory will fill the earth. And God's kingdom will last forever.

But the story does not end there. In some ways, a new story will just be beginning.

CHAPTER TEN

So, what do you think?

Now that you know the story, you must decide something. It is the same thing everyone who has ever heard the story must decide. Do you believe that the story is true? Will you decide to follow Jesus?

Most people can see that the world is not like God intended it to be. The world is broken, and we are broken too. We do things that are not good. We think thoughts that are not good. We say things that hurt other people. Like Adam and Eve, we have not honored the God who made us.

But God loves us, and he has chosen to have mercy on us. God has made a way for us to be right with him. But we must believe that Jesus is the Son of God. We must believe that, on the cross, Jesus gave his life in order to save ours. We must trust in who Jesus is and what he has done for us. We must believe that he died and is alive again. We must turn from our sin. We must believe in Jesus and trust his words.

When we put our trust in Jesus, God will forgive us for the evil things that we have done. And then he will give us new life. He will give us his Holy Spirit to help us live it. That is God's **promise**.

But following Jesus will not be easy. Satan does not want you to honor God. Many people did not like what Jesus said when he was here. Some people hated him so much that they wanted to kill him. When you follow Jesus, some people may be angry with you. They may even hate you as they hated Jesus. But if you follow Jesus, he will always be with you to help you.

Now that you know the story, you have a choice to make. You can decide to live the way you have always lived. You can believe what you have always believed. You can trust that your way is the best way to live. Or you can believe that the story of Jesus is true. Jesus is the Son of God. He lived and died and came to life again to rescue people like you. The only way to be right with God is through Jesus.

> If you follow Jesus, he will always be with you to help you.

CHAPTER ELEVEN

What can you do?

Do you believe that the story of Jesus is true?
Do you want to follow him?
Here is what you can do.

Talk to God

The first thing to do when you believe is talk to God. He listens. He has known you since you were born. You have never said a word that he did not hear. So, speak to him. Thank him for his great love for you. Tell God that you know that you have done many things that do not please him. You need God to show you mercy. But you cannot earn the mercy that you need.

Believe and accept that what he said is true and trust Jesus to rescue you. Ask God to help you turn away from your sin. Ask God to forgive you and welcome you into his family. You could use words like these to talk to God:

> *Dear God,*
>
> *I know that I have done many wrong things that do not please you. I did not know you or follow you. Please forgive me.*
>
> *Thank you for loving me. Thank you for sending your Son to die for people like me so that I could be forgiven. Thank you for bringing Jesus back to life. I ask you to give me a new life too.*
>
> *I now submit to Jesus as my ruler and Lord. Help me to turn away from the things that do not please you. Please help me to be the person that you made me to be.*
>
> *Amen.*

Follow Jesus

Start by learning what Jesus said and doing what Jesus did. Talk to God often. Ask God to be with you and guide you in his ways. Ask God to help you see the things in your life that need to change. You may have old habits that do not honor God. Maybe you are angry or selfish or you have hurt other people. Ask God to change those bad things and make new habits that honor him. Ask God to make you kind and patient. Ask him to give you courage to follow him in every way.

If you do not have a Bible, ask God to help you find one. Read the Scriptures. As you read the Bible, God will show you how to live. God will use those words to make you wise. He will use his word to guide you when you do not know what to do. He will use those words to make you strong when you need help.

Look for other people who follow Jesus. We call people who gather to worship Jesus, the church. Be baptized. Baptism is a sign that you trust Jesus and have become one of his people. These people are like your brothers and sisters in the family of God. Meet with them. Learn from them. Pray with them. You cannot follow Jesus well if you try to do it alone. God expects us to depend on one another and encourage one another as we follow Jesus.

Keep Trusting

Never forget that you are right with God because of what Jesus did for you. Not because of what you have done for him. It is important to remember this. We will not be perfect even when we trust God and do our best. We will sometimes do things that do not please God. We may forget to love as we should or fall back into a bad habit. When we do, we must ask God to forgive us and change us. We must continue to trust in the work that Jesus has done for us.

God starts his work to make us more like Jesus when we believe. And we can trust him to continue that good work in us. And he will until we go to be with Jesus or when Jesus comes again to be with us. That is a **promise**.

Would you like to learn more about God's story?

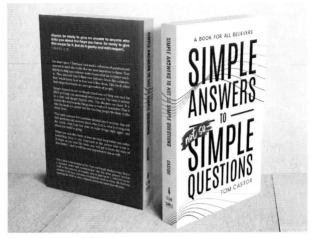

You can download this free book, *Simple Answers to not so Simple Questions* at asimpleword.org/downloads/

A Simple Word

To connect with us, visit www.asimpleword.org
We would be glad to help.